Streeters

Rants and Raves from
This Hour Has 22 Minutes

Rick Mercer

Foreword by Peter Gzowski

Seal Books
Toronto

STREETERS
A Seal Book
Doubleday Canada paperback edition published in 1998
Seal edition April 1999

For information: Seal Books, 105 Bond Street,
Toronto, Ontario M5B 1Y3

ISBN 0-7704-2837-1

Cover design: Janine Laporte
Cover photograph: Rino Noto

Seal Books are published by Doubleday Canada
Limited. Its trademark, consisting of the words "Seal
Books" and the portrayal of a seal, is the property of
Doubleday Canada Limited, 105 Bond Street, Toronto,
Ontario M5B 1Y3, Canada. This trademark has been
duly registered in the Trademark Office of Canada.

PRINTED AND BOUND IN CANADA

UNI 10 9 8 7 6 5 4 3 2 1

For Ken and Pat Mercer

Acknowledgements

The "streeters" have all been directed for television by Henry Sarwer-Foner. The man who shoots them is Peter Sutherland. Anything I can do he can do better and backwards. Kenny MacDonald made sure the words stuck to the tape.

I am indebted to the "talented and ever so lovely" Helen Pelham, *22 Minutes* Editorial Producer Geoff D'Eon and, of course, Mary Walsh, Greg Thomey and Cathy Jones.

A special thank you to my literary agent, Suzanne DePoe; Susan MacDonald, Kim Ross, Karen Byers, and Patti Parsons at *22 Minutes*; Michael Donovan and everyone at Salter Street Films; Phyllis Platt, George Anthony, Jack Kellum, and everyone on the CBC crew in Halifax.

All of these "streeters" were originally edited for television by *22 Minutes* Creative Producer Gerald Lunz, who more often than not was responsible for taking a long rambling script and creating something funny that could be performed in less than two minutes. Thank you.

Author's Note

About six years ago I started yelling at a TV camera once a week, and I haven't shut up since.

Fortunately, the people who run this country have provided me with no shortage of subjects to shout about.

These are not columns, they're rants.

Feel free to read them out loud, very loud, and rant along.

Rick Mercer

Foreword

by Peter Gzowski

My daughter Alison discovered him long before I did. She was living and working in St. John's, one place where she could catch on at CBC Radio without someone saying she was just riding my flapping coat-tails, and, like anyone else of any sensibility in that city, she was spending as much time as she could in the audience at the Longshoremen's Protective Union Hall. The LSPU, as everyone calls it, ought to have a plaque in honour of the number of theatrical careers — nearly all of them comedic theatrical careers — that have been launched there over the years, from Mary Walsh and Greg Malone and Cathy and Andy Jones to (the now late, alas) Tommy Sexton, to, well, almost everyone from Newfoundland who's ever made you laugh, which is, come to think of it, a heck of a long list.

Alison saw Rick Mercer at the LSPU when he was, she thinks, about eighteen, in a revue called Corey and Wade's. He'd already flung himself into theatre at high school, under the tutelage of his drama teacher Lois Brown (who later went on to program the LSPU), and as soon as Alison saw him, she said to me on the phone one day, she knew she'd seen brilliance. She had him record one of his pieces for the radio, but the CBC, in its wisdom, declined to air it, even though Rick took the naughtiest words out.

From there, with the help of Ottawa producer Gerald Lunz (who went on to become creative producer of *This Hour Has 22 Minutes*), Rick began writing and performing his one-man plays — three of them, in all, that took him from St. John's to Vancouver to enthusiastic reviews.

Although I (or my voice) appeared in one of those plays — Rick's character, I think, was taking over radio — our paths still didn't cross until *22 Minutes* was well underway. At Alison's urging, I invited him to open one of the evenings we hold at the old Red Barn theatre in Jackson's Point, Ontario, to raise money for literacy. It's the night before our golf tournament.

To tell you the truth, I had some trepidation. Rick can, after all, be pretty hard-edged, and our audience at the Red Barn in the cottage country of Lake Simcoe — who pay $100 a pop for their tickets — are not exactly hip, downtown Toronto types.

I needn't have worried. Rick was fabulous. He worked very hard on his six-minute piece (when we talked afterward I saw some ballpoint notes on the palm of his hand), and even now, when we've had more than a hundred acts at the Barn over eight years, people still talk about his cheeky but astute comments on literacy, and on his passage about baby boomers (there's a version of it in this book, by the way) and its memorable "We don't give a shit *where* you were when Kennedy was killed."

I've had the pleasure of doing a couple of things with Rick since. He's called me up from *22 Minutes* and talked me into (1) being interviewed at the East Coast Music Awards, where he asked me if it was true I'd called Perrin Beatty, the president of the CBC, a son of a bitch, and, when I confessed, asked if there were any other people I'd like to get at, and, when I offered him a list that ran from Rex Murphy to Mr. Dressup, put most of it on the air, and (2) going on a mock pub crawl with him in Halifax, which ended up with the two of us in a tattoo parlour and, later, in jail. "He's got the Order of Canada, you know," Rick yelled from our cell in the closing scene.

Well, actually, that was J.B. Dickson, Rick's reportorial persona.

Yet it was Rick, too — totally original, as quick as a politician's turnabout, saying the unsayable, but, as often as not, saying what we all might have said if only we had the nerve — or, of course, the wit. Alison was right all along. He's a bloody genius, and we're lucky to have him among us.

Streeters

Rants and Raves from
This Hour Has 22 Minutes

It's My Party,
But It's Not Official

(First aired October 8, 1993)

To be considered an official, bona fide party in this election you need fifty candidates in fifty ridings, at a thousand dollars per. That's fifty thousand bucks. So having a Bloc Ontario is possible, and a Bloc Québécois is no sweat, but what about the rest of us? We don't have fifty ridings.

In Canada, some provinces are far more equal than others. When you're a kid, you say, "Dad, how come I have to come home when the streetlights come on and Todd doesn't?" And Dad says, "'Cuz Todd's bigger, now go to your room." That may be the way to raise children, but it's not the way to run a country.

This new policy has already had a lot of casualties. The Communist Party of Canada is no longer a real party. That's not right. Communists are real people too — stupid people, sure, but they're real. This means we can no longer scream "Move to China" at the local Communist candidate. And, hey, yelling at communists is my constitutional right.

If someone wants to start a Vancouver Central Separatist Party and wants to give Kim Campbell a run for her money, I say put his party on the ballot and more power to 'em.

All major religions started out as cults, and all major parties started out with fewer than fifty candidates. And although the powers that be mightn't realize it, a fifty-thousand-dollar cover charge on democracy is too much money. I say all Canadians should get in free with the band.

It'll Never Happen

(First aired October 15, 1993)

We live in the most helplessly democratic country in the world. We're well on the way to having a separatist becoming leader of Her Majesty's Loyal Opposition.

That job comes with a few perks. The salary, for starters — 113,000 bucks a year. A whack of servants. And, of course, the house, Stornoway, a thirty-eight-room mansion built in 1913.

And who owns this house? We do, the taxpayers, we are the landlords. So it is in my capacity as landlord of Stornoway that I raise these concerns. What will the Bloc Québécois do with historic Stornoway? If they want to destroy the country, can they be trusted with the rugs? Are the Bloc going to take their shoes off on the front porch?

I say that if the Bloc becomes the Official Opposition, we should get a damage deposit and the equivalent of first and last months' rent. Someone goes in there with a video camera and a Polaroid and documents any stain or blemish in the place. If they so much as touch the curtains or move a plant, give 'em their notice and the whole lot of them can rent a place at the Château Laurier.

Let them destroy the country on their own dime.

Attention, Woolworths Shoppers

(First aired November 1, 1993)

So the management of Woolworths has a big problem on their hands.

One of the big factors in the Woolworth success story is a middle class, and as far as Woolworth executives are concerned, we don't have a middle class any more, so thirteen thousand jobs are on the line. They're gonna close half their stores and open boutiques for rich people and they're gonna turn the other half into bargain huts. No more middle class — no more Woolworths. Where are the men in this country gonna go to buy socks? We are set in our ways.

If there has ever been a time for government intervention in private business, this is it. This must be Jean Chrétien's number-one order of business. Because, I tell you, I've got a nose for disaster, and one of these days men and women in this country are gonna wake up in desperate need of hosiery and when they find out the store is closed there is gonna be anarchy and bloodshed nationwide.

I'm seeing angry, stick-waving, sockless mobs gunning for the prime minister's head. So c'mon, Jean, never mind the helicopters, never mind the Bloc, we're dying out here without a middle class — we're screwed!

Where Were You When You Heard the Story for the Hundredth Time?

(First aired November 17, 1993)

Every time I turn around some baby boomer is talking about Generation X. Baby boomers love being baby boomers, but they can't handle for one minute that our generation doesn't have a name attached to it.

Don't get me wrong, it's not that we're not endlessly fascinated to hear where you were when JFK died. I know, I know. So you were sitting in class. The nun came in. She was crying. She said the president's been shot and you have the day off school. Wow. That's amazing. That exact same thing only happened to about 500 million people. And we're really sorry about how you all had to go through the whole Cuban missile crisis thing. It's just that we never lived it; we skimmed it in grade eight, but we didn't live it.

See, we're not like baby boomers, we have no common denominators. There's no defining moment that has galvanized us as a whole. Okay, sure, we all know where we were when Kurt Cobain died. But that doesn't count.

So, the next time you see a baby boomer on late-night television saying, "Coming up next . . . 'What Is Generation X?' " just pity the poor fella and take whatever he has to say with a grain of salt. It's all lies, and anyways, baby boomers — they should all be in bed.

Nervous About NAFTA

(First aired November 24, 1993)

I don't want to claim that I'm an international trade expert here, but I do think that any worries that Canadians have about NAFTA are completely unnecessary.

Canadian jobs are not going to Mexico. I happen to know for a fact that having a large workforce that will work for nothing and a government that will turn a blind eye to environmental regulations does not — I repeat, does not — mean that big business will flock your way overnight. If that were the case, where are all the textile plants in Newfoundland? Last time I looked, I could be wrong here, Atlantic Canada wasn't exactly stealing all the car-manufacturing jobs on the continent.

So Mexico or no, everything stays the same. People in Central Canada have nothing to worry about, and people in the regions have nothing to look forward to. What we *do* have is a $40-billion deficit and a hard winter coming.

So just forget about NAFTA, get your wood in, put the plastic up to the windows, batten down the hatches, and relax!

Christmas Tan

(First aired December 6, 1993)

This Christmas, like every Christmas before it, will see Canadians travelling en masse from one icy locale to another to be close to friends and loved ones.

'Tis the season to be with your family and friends. 'Tis the season to ponder why it is that for the cost of flying five feet within Canada you can fly to Florida, get a hotel, a rental car, and free drinks for a week.

If there was a God, the minister of transport would step in now and halt all flights to sunspots over the holidays. And Canadians who try to beat the system by slipping over to Buffalo for a cheap flight south — try 'em for treason.

And for the month of January, wherever it is illegal now to have a smoke it would be illegal to have a tan. If a co-worker walks in the office the first week of January showing off his tan line, we will band together and shout "unclean, unclean!" We'll give the tanned the worst seats in restaurants, make them stand outside in freezing rain. It'll give us regular old pasty-faced Canadians from sea to shining sea a chance to stand together united, mocking the sunbaked.

We're After Gaining!

(First aired January 10, 1994)

The average Canadian gained five pounds over Christmas, and there's twenty-five million people in Canada, which means Canada became 125 million pounds heavier over the holidays. And if I'm any indication of an average Canadian, half of that was caused by gravy. As far as deciding on New Year's Eve that you're going to lose it all and have a washboard stomach by March Break — give it up, can't be done.

But smokers are the worst. Go to a government building the first week of January, hundreds of people out in sixty-below windchill cutting the extra-long filters off the extra-long cigarettes, praying for a Rothmans like they used to smoke.

The secret is to make resolutions that we *can* keep — Canadian resolutions. Like I'm not going to cut meat out of my diet but I will cut the gravy intake by . . . half. I'm not going to plan a cardio-vascular activity for every weekend, but . . . I will get out of bed by noon. I will not stop drinking alto-gether, but I will explore light beer . . . as a lunchtime beverage, at least for now. I've been doing it for years.

Protect Your Parts

(First aired January 17, 1994)

There are at present over five hundred men's groups in this country — not counting poker games. Just men sitting around talking about men's issues — and there are many.

We have our own cycles, we've got a lot of stress in our lives. We need more sleep than women, we're only comfortable in track pants, we're not very good at puzzles, and we're three and a half times more likely to end up in a mental institution.

And as far as I was concerned, that was fine. That's just part of what psychologists are now calling the burden of being male. We were put on this Earth to suffer, and we accept that. It's manly.

But now it's gone too far. There is nothing — I repeat, nothing — funny about a sleeping man waking up with no penis. When I think of that poor man waking up like that, praying that the only thing under those sheets was a horse's head and an offer he couldn't refuse . . . but no, and now he's the laughingstock of the First World.

And every woman on the planet thinks she should get off scot-free. But I tell you, if that lady walks, there will be dire consequences, indeed. Men the world over will haul off the choke chain and run for the hills and the L.A. riots will look like a walk in the park, because holl hath no fury like a man torn.

Move East

(First aired January 24, 1994)

I don't know, call me crazy, call me a coward, but what person in their right mind would live in Los Angeles?

What comes to mind when you think of Los Angeles? Riots. Fires. Six cops beating a man within an inch of his life. Three guys dropping a rock on another guy's head. Four feet of water rushing down your street while hellfire comes straight out of the ground, burning your car and house in under three minutes.

And if that's not bad enough, apparently Liona Boyd lives there.

I'm from Newfoundland. People say, "Why do you live in Newfoundland?" We say, "Why do you live in Toronto?" But, c'mon, we all have our reasons why we prefer to be in one region of Canada over the others.

Really, God love Canada. How often do any of us here wake up with a nine-hundred-pound mahogany dresser-drawer heading towards our face at warp speed?

We've got it scald. We have every right in the world to be holier than thou when it comes to the flaky state of California. Except for the crowd in B.C., who, yes, even though the tulips come up in February, and the quality of life is apparently two thousand times greater than ours, they too are just sitting there eating sushi waiting for the Big One.

People have their priorities mixed up, and I think the events of the last little while have proven that everyone should stop moving west and move east. Sure, it's more tundra-like than Vancouver. And granted, we don't have celebrities walking the streets, but at least when we hear someone saying "The Big One is coming" we know they're probably talking about the WWF show at the hockey arena. You might still want to run and hide, but you don't have to. The choice is yours.

So come east, young man and woman, come east. It mightn't be as warm, but at least it's not gonna kill you.

Liar, Liar, Pants on Fire

(First aired February 7, 1994)

Jag Bhaduria gets elected as a Liberal member of Parliament, but then they find out that he lied about his law degree and wrote threatening letters to his employer, the Toronto School Board. Now people are saying that there should be legislation passed that would force him to resign.

I sympathize with them, but are they mad? Do people actually think that it's practical that a politician would be fired for lying? Be wary of what you wish for. There would be a by-election every other week in every other Canadian riding. Forget going to the cottage or having a social life, we'd spend half our lives inside a ballot box.

If anyone is to blame here, it's the media for not catching Jag Bhaduria's phoney credentials in the first place. The nation's watchdogs, the Eric

Mallings of Canada, were asleep at the wheel. And the crowd in Markham, Ontario, are stuck with an MP who's a bit loose with the truth and has a reputation for making bizarre statements.

That's hardly a unique situation. I was stuck with John Crosbie for the last seventeen years. Every month, "Dear Constituent, The fish stocks are growing like gangbusters and Sheila Copps should lie down and love me again."

Yes, dear Markhamites, just like John, all things, including Mr. Bhaduria, will pass.

Steal This Book

(First aired February 14, 1994)

Since time immemorial people have tried to figure out how to reduce taxes. Well, obviously the solution has been staring us in the face. Steal, defraud, and smuggle.

Clyde Wells, an avid anti-smoker himself, agreed to the federal government's lowering of cigarette taxes. He says he did it "in the name of national unity." He said no to Meech Lake but he's all for this. He must have some romantic notion about all of us coughing up blood together from sea to shining sea.

But, hey, if it works for cigarette taxes, it should work for everything. Nobody files their income tax on time, and they'll have to lower that too. Instead of buying liquor, steal it! When they yell, "Halt, police!" you shout "Can't, b'y, too much tax" on the way out the door. And don't buy a new car, steal one.

If we steal everything, taxes will lower and we will actually leave a tax-free Canada for generations to come.

Of course, we'd be hurtling towards out-and-out anarchy at a pretty fast pace, but, hey, at least part of me thinks that anarchy is probably not all that bad. Perhaps we could have a system of anarchy with no taxes but lots of rules — and a police force — and municipal upkeep of water and sewers — and health care . . . but that's it. Okay, maybe UIC — and job retraining — and, oh, God, I suppose we'd have to pay for it all somehow.

Hey, I've got an idea! How about everyone who smokes cigarettes will have to pay a tariff? Say about $1,100 a pack. There's only five and a half million smokers in Canada — that should do it.

Death Stars
Are a Good Thing

(First aired February 21, 1994)

Every time you turn on the TV now, there's a panel of experts talking about death stars and the five-hundred-channel universe. And they always ask the question, "Do we really need five hundred TV channels?" What a stupid question!

Has anyone ever said, "Do we really need five hundred books in the library?" No. Of course, if you ask anyone over the age of forty do they want five hundred channels, you know they'll say no, they still haven't figured out how to set their VCR. They're the same people who think the answering machine is broken when the tape runs out.

To them, five hundred channels just means yet another remote control that they will never, ever understand. To me, five hundred channels means we're five hundred steps closer to cracking the secrets of the universe. I think that's beautiful.

Will people watch all these specialty channels? The weather channel is doing well, who would have guessed, and God knows, enough people have sat back in their pyjamas and drunk beer while watching TV experts talk about how there's too much TV on TV.

I'd say that if the Three's Company channel was up and running, there'd be a pretty good chance they'd turn over to have a quick look at Suzanne Somers fall over the couch a few times.

That's good television!

Our Saviour, Mr. Axworthy

(First aired March 14, 1994)

If you're between fifteen and twenty-five, your prayers have been answered. Lloyd Axworthy loves the youth. He eats, drinks, and sleeps the youth.

Lloyd says that he is daring the young to dream and now he's whispered the words that young people have been eager to hear since the beginning of time: opportunity incentives. Now, anyone who's house-trained a puppy knows all about *opportunity incentives*. They mean that all of you people who slog like a trained monkey at Dairy Queen and accrue personal debts that rival a Third World country, in the noble pursuit of higher education, you're out of luck. The gravy train is over, mister, you've had it too good.

Lloyd Axworthy says you need incentives. Lloyd, we've got incentives. It's because we're realists, and we have a dream, a recurring dream. It's the year 2035. We're sixty-odd years old and we're leaning across a counter and saying, "Do you want fries with that, young man?"

That's the incentive, Lloyd. So drop the high-school speaking tours, forget fancy "youth incentive 1994" reports. What people need is opportunity, plain old. Give 'em some of that and they might dare to dream after all.

On the Backs
of the Youth

(First aired March 18, 1994)

The Government of Canada has actually said they
will guarantee employment to young people — provided they give up their rights to social assistance.
Was that a Liberal government we elected?

A minute ago Jean Chrétien was giving hope back
to the people. Now he's applying the War
Measures Act to the unemployment problem.

What, is he nuts? If we're gonna start taking away
people's rights, let's take a few sacred perks in
the process. Like, say, the pensions of the two
hundred MPs who were kicked out of office last
year. There's a few bucks to be saved there.
What's the current payoff for a big fat loser in
Canada? John Turner gets eighty-five grand a year,
if that's any indication. And Joe Clark? Prime minister for five minutes and the man in charge of

national unity. The country is nearly bankrupt, a separatist party is the Official Opposition, and he gets eighty-two grand a year? I'm not saying we take away their right to go down in history as losers, let's just take away the salary.

Let's put it to a vote. Should we pay $15 million a year to MPs we just fired, or should we ask people to give up their rights for minimum wage? Oh, yeah, that's a path we want to wander down. What's next? If we give up our right to see a lawyer, we won't get punched in the head?

Back to the drawing board, boys. With Liberals like these, who needs Conservatives? You're starting to make Preston Manning look like a humanitarian, for godsakes!

Foot in Mouth

(First aired March 21, 1994)

The Reform Party was put on the spot again this week. Their immigration critic has suggested that Jamaicans were the ones responsible for rising crime in Toronto. When in doubt, blame the visible minorities.

And what did Preston do? He came to his member's defence by saying that, and I quote, he was just "calling a spade a spade."

"Calling a spade a spade," Mr. Manning? Did you choose those words carefully or did they just come tumbling off the old tongue?

What is going on with the Reform Party? I mean, have they been to school at all? Didn't they have mothers? "If you don't have anything nice to say then don't say anything at all." Didn't they get hugged enough when they were young?

Because there's definitely a few little dos and don'ts that Reformers don't seem to be aware of. Little things like don't quote Adolf Hitler in your newsletters, a lot of people don't like Hitler very much. Don't go complaining that too many French people speak French, it's just a stupid thing to say. Don't use the word "spade" when blaming Jamaicans for crime. Actually, I take that back. Don't even bother blaming Jamaicans for crime. And, last but not least, if you're the leader of a political party, please insure that at least some of your members are up off all fours. It makes it easier come election time.

Our National Shame

(First aired March 28, 1994)

We've gone too far this time. We've really blown it. The Germans are very upset with us. The Germans have done some pretty awful things in their time, but as far as they're concerned, Canadians have taken the cake.

Our loggers won't quit logging. Our hunters won't quit hunting. And word on the street is that our gatherers won't stop gathering. The list goes on and on. And if that's not bad enough, even the cast of *Beverly Hills 90210* are upset because our Natives won't stop trapping.

If we keep carrying on like this, people are going to start thinking that we're a country filled with northern people or something.

If only that whole crowd of hunters and gatherers would just come to their senses. Really, why don't they leave just wherever it is these people who live off the land live and come to the city? Where people really care about the issues, where there's blue boxes and benefit concerts with great bands who have cool hair. It's a black-and-white issue if I ever saw one. Live off the land — bad. Live off the city — good.

And God love the Germans and the kids from Beverly Hills High for showing us the error of our ways.

Queen of the Little People

(First aired October 17, 1994)

Roseanne Skoke, Liberal MP for Central Nova, hates homosexuals. She says she's normal, but they're statistically abnormal.

Well, you know, it depends on how you look at these things, doesn't it? I mean, speaking of statistical abnormalities, how many four-foot-five female members of Parliament are there in Canada? Not many. I'd guess . . . one.

I hope all the tall non-members of Parliament don't get together and have a vote about short people in Parliament, or short people in general, for that matter.

I mean, if they want to be short, fine, but give 'em an inch and they'll take a mile. Next thing, they'll be saying they can't be fired for being short, and

38

they'll want to get married to other short people, have short children, the whole shebang. It's just not fair to tall people.

And you know, Roseanne, it's not like I don't know what I'm talking about. I've never admitted this before, but I once experimented . . . with being . . . short, but then I realized that being a short grown man was unnatural, immoral, and perhaps a threat to Canadian families.

So Roseanne, I think you should just do what I did. Do what Svend Robinson did. When we were four feet tall we made a conscious lifestyle decision to keep growing. And if you're not up to the challenge physically, Roseanne, you should really consider it mentally.

Chrétien in China

(First aired November 21, 1994)

I wish people would just get off Jean Chrétien's
back. The man goes to China, he makes a few
deals, makes us a pile of cash, and what happens? Everyone is all up in arms just because of
a few minor human rights violations. Look,
Chrétien has no choice.

My next-door neighbour and I, we go halves on fire-
wood, I save money. It's a great deal for me. But
there's some soft-left liberals out there who
would prefer I didn't even talk to the man.

Okay, so he ran over a couple of kids in his car
because they were making a racket out on the
cul-de-sac. And, yes, he's got a bunch of youngsters chained to the furnace because they talked
back.

But hey, it's not like I haven't made my feelings
known to the man. I've done my part. One time I

said, "That's bad." He changed the topic, we went on with our business, had a beer, whatever.

My conscience is clear, and like Jean Chrétien I cannot afford to jeopardize this very special, mutually-profitable relationship with my learned neighbour just because of a few people chained up in his basement.

And don't give me any grief here. Hey, I'm only following my prime minister's lead.

Nice Odds,
If They Were Ours

(First aired December 19, 1994)

Jacques Parizeau is like a man possessed. He's a man with a mission, he's a force to be reckoned with, and, yes, he's got a plan.

And what do we have? Who's leading the pro-Canada forces? Who's gonna convince the Québécois to keep this country together? Daniel Johnson, that's who.

Johnson versus Parizeau: it's like pitting a hamster against a pit bull. It's so typically Canadian that the future of this country is in the hands of a guy whose claim to fame is the ability to lull thousands of people into a deep, dark REM sleep every time he opens his mouth. And not only that, he's the son of a premier, and let's face it, people don't like sons of premiers.

And during the referendum, people in Quebec will have to decide either to side with the man with the plan, the man who took his party from nothing and swept the province in the last election, or to play follow the loser, vote for the dullard and stay in Canada.

Why have a referendum at all? Why not just give Parizeau the keys to the country? Say, "Open her up and go mad, Jacques, take whatever you want. We won't stop you, we won't even flinch, because that would be downright un-Canadian."

New Year's Eve Already ... Again?

(First aired January 9, 1995)

One week into 1995 and all bets are off. We've blown every resolution we made.

I know, you're like me, we woke up after Christmas, we drove down to Super Bodies, parked the car, went indoors, took the tour, plunked down the plastic for a twelve-month membership. Guess what? We're never gonna set foot inside the building again.

And we all stopped drinking. Of course we did — we almost died on New Year's Eve. The light at the end of the tunnel was a paramedic. But we're over that now, and what's Friday without a few beers? We're back to square one.

The problem is we should stop giving up things we're already hooked on. Let's face it: smoking cigarettes and speaking in tongues, once you start you'll never stop.

Learn to love your old habits and resolve not to start new ones, good or bad. To succeed in the New Year.

Glass Houses

(First aired January 23, 1995)

When I was in grade four I woke up and heard Peter Gzowski say that the Canadian dollar was worth seventy-five cents. I freaked out, took everything I had, eight bucks in change, and bought forty-six fudgesticks at recess.

I was hedging my bets against inflation. I panicked. I suffered. Half the fudgesticks melted and I ended up with an ice cream headache.

And now, twenty years later, the dollar's back down, the debt's up, and everyone's freaking out because the *Wall Street Journal* says we're an honorary member of the Third World. The pain is coming back.

Okay, let's not be rash. Stay off the fudgesticks. We're the Third World? Says who? The *Wall Street Journal*. And where in the world do they live? New York City, one of the biggest sewers on the face of the earth.

My advice to the crowd south of the border: people who live in glass outhouses shouldn't throw stones. Otherwise, we'll just start flinging them right back at ya.

We'll go toe to toe with the Yanks on guns, crime, Florida, air, water, medicare, and the biggest advantage that we've got of them all: at least we're not Americans.

No Revolution, Please, We're Canadian

(First aired February 6, 1995)

So we're gonna have a tax revolt, are we? So we're gonna rise up and say "no more taxes." We're gonna tell Paul Martin that the country won't take it anymore. No ifs, ands, or buts about it this time, we're just gonna say no.

No, no, we're not! Look at the GST. Not one car was torched, no windows were broken. No great hordes were hauled off to jail. And look at the students now. Ottawa calls them our country's greatest natural resource. And what's gonna happen? Their tuition is going to double. *Double*. Times two. They're screwed. They've got nothing to lose, they're up against a wall, and what did they do? Ten percent marched in the streets and the remaining ninety percent stayed indoors. They didn't want to leave their class. Let's face it. The closest we come to a revolution is when someone wins the Stanley Cup.

So when this budget comes down, who will lead us in this revolt? Who will be Canada's own Che Guevara? No one, that's who, and Paul Martin knows it. He can do whatever he wants. He can raise taxes, he can double tuition, he can even shoot Bambi's mom if he wants to, and we'll just go about our business. And if wo can't say anything nice about the budget, we won't say anything at all.

Company Is Coming

(First aired February 13, 1995)

The prime minister was in Halifax recently. He was giving a personal prime-ministerial once-over on the big plans for the big G-7. Twenty-four hundred journalists and all the other leaders in the industrialized world will be in Halifax for a three-day summit in June.

And so they should. Canada is a great country. Halifax is a good city, and it's got a great big building with a great big swanky boardroom overlooking something most of them don't have — a modern old-world harbour.

It's a good thing that way back in 1988 the federal government had the foresight to say they would clean up the harbour.

Oh, right, I forgot. No sooner was the ink dry on that deal than they changed their mind and decided that the harbour wasn't worth it.

And now the same people who said no to a 1988 cleanup have a brand-new number-one 1995 priority. Company's coming. Hide the sewage, cover it in balloons, hide it with a banner, divert it to another part of the city: that's the plan.

Who raised the federal government? Somewhere along the line most people figured out that if Mom tells you to clean up your room 'cuz company's coming, you'd better do a good job or else.

You've got five months, Jean. Start cleaning and smarten up. Yes, one of those twenty-four hundred journalists might just look under the bed.

Smile!

(First aired February 27, 1995)

When you think about what inventions have completely altered society, a couple of biggies top the list. There's fire, the wheel, the fridge, and so on.

But in recent time, the one invention that really sticks out is obvious. The easy-to-use, two-pound, hand-held home video camera. Before videos, we had to be content just to hear about how cute our nephews were at their grade three French immersion Christmas concert. Now we get to watch all two and a half hours. And they say vacation slide shows were bad. Videotapes are six hours long and there's no hope in hell the bulb will ever burn out.

But before video, if you were asked, "Who ya gonna believe, the low-down, lying, good-for-nothing nobody or the one who has taken an oath to serve and protect?" you wouldn't be blamed for pickin' the latter.

But now it turns out that every time there's a video camera around, the low-down, lying, good-for-nothing nobodies are being whacked with sticks on the L.A. freeway, rode around like donkeys by a bunch of Airborno, or having their clothes cut off by a 911 tool-wielding riot squad compliments of the women's pen. Which is, I've been told, even worse than watching your nephew's grade three French immersion Christmas concert.

But if you ever find yourself on the wrong end of a nightstick, you'll thank your lucky stars if someone somewhere has you perfectly framed with that easy-to-use, dummy-proof auto-focus and zoom.

Will You Know My Name?

(First aired March 6, 1995)

God love the baby boomers. If it wasn't for the baby boom, where would young people be today? What would the future hold? God knows, but they might have a job for starters. Never mind having a hope in hell of ever seeing a pension.

Baby boomers did it all. They got all the jobs. They keep the jobs. And when they leave their jobs, their jobs are cancelled, leaving no jobs behind. And then with the longest life expectancy of any group since the beginning of time, they're gonna gallivant along and collect a pension until the pension plan is broke or they're all 106 — whichever comes first.

And where does that leave anyone born after 1962? Sitting around with no job, no future, reading yet another *Rolling Stone* cover story about a fifty-five-year-old drug-addled rock star on his "After the Liver Transplant" comeback tour.

Yes, there's a special place in heaven for baby boomers. The only upside is they'll all die before we do and then they'll have to wait thirty or forty years until we get there to flip their burgers and fetch them their fries.

My Hero—This Week

(First aired March 13, 1995)

Every night on the news, there's constant mind-numbing information about global interest rates. We have to sit there and watch thousands of money traders screaming at the tops of their lungs in a language nobody understands.

And just when you think it's completely incomprehensible and dull as dishwater, along comes a shining light — a twenty-eight-year-old Brit who failed his grade eleven algebra exam pushes a few buttons, bankrupts a bank, and loses a billion bucks in the process. Now, that *is* exciting.

Because of Nick Leeson, the Queen of England herself thought she was going to lose millions from her personal fortune. I think that's great. I say, "Buy the man a beer." Talk about your YTV Young Persons Achievement Award candidate.

Do you know how many bags of money Bonnie and

Clyde would have had to steal before they could lose a billion bucks? And everyone says, "How could it happen? How could Nick Leeson have so much power?" You thought he was hot before he lost the billion, wait till he gets out. Never mind the Wealthy Barber — wait until the Busted Banker hits the lecture circuit, with *How to Make or Break a Billion Bucks with Everyone Else's Money.* I'd buy it.

Harris in Heaven

(First aired October 16, 1995)

So Mike Harris is the brand-new premier of Ontario. Of course, he wasn't always a politician. He used to be a golf pro. But he learned a lot when he was a golf pro. He learned . . . how to play golf. And somewhere he learned about injustice.

Mike sees that the Royal Bank and other Ontario companies have to pay an annual fifty-dollar corporate filing fee and Mike says: "That's not right." Mike sees youngsters and the elderly with lung disease getting free oxygen at home and Mike says: "That's not right." So he gives the bank a fifty-dollar break and takes ten million bucks from the home oxygen program. Then he goes out and plays golf.

And between rounds he pops up and says the future unfortunate residents of Ontario will have to turn to the church in times of need. And it's funny that he brings up church, because people who go to church believe in God. And people who believe in God believe in heaven. And people who believe in heaven know that if you take away someone's oxygen you're not getting in.

But then again, it's hardly a revolutionary idea. It's just Common Sense.

This Country
Has Seven Days

(First aired October 23, 1995)

In exactly one week we will know if Quebec is gonna file for divorce. One week and the country as we know it may cease to exist. And what's The Plan? Nothing. That's The Plan, according to Ottawa. Do nothing and leave it up to Daniel Johnson. Leave it up to a man who makes Joe Clark look like Liberace.

What's Johnson gonna do? Tell people to vote no or he'll bore them to death? And who do the separatists have? Lucien Bouchard, and he's the most dangerous type of politician there is. He's the type who figures if he can turn Quebec into a country he's just that far from turning water into wine.

And where's the prime minister through all this? He's been so busy applying hickeys to the arses of Asian dictators, it's a wonder he knows what's going on in his own country. C'mon, Jean, time to haul out the stops, buddy. This Country Has Seven Days.

Close Enough
For Ya?

(First aired November 6, 1995)

Okay, so the ballots have been counted, and we came away the winners, but, let's face it, the numbers are just a bit too close for comfort. Maybe the time has come where we swallow our pride, suck it back, and say, "Yes, yes, yes, boy, yes, you're a distinct society."

Who cares what Quebec's called? It's not like anyone else other than Clyde Wells is actually gonna read the bloody Constitution. Quebec could be called the one-eyed oogly-boogly monster for all I care.

I know people say, no, if you call them distinct you're saying they're special and that means we're no longer equal. Yes, well, you could also say if you call them distinct you're saying they're special, and special also means, you know, special, which also means we're no longer equal. Whatever way you look at it, let's just do the deed, put it behind us, and get on with the business of running if not the greatest, the most dysfunctional, country on the face of the planet.

Terror at 24 Sussex

(First aired November 13, 1995)

Jean Chrétien has just taken "doing nothing" to a whole new level.

It is one thing to do nothing while a crazy person is out beating the band to destroy the country. But, c'mon, Jean . . . when there's a crazy person out beating down the door of your house with a rock, you might want to at least get out of bed. But no, what did he do? He rolls over and goes back to sleep.

See, he figured there was only a fifty-fifty chance the crazy person would actually succeed, and he sleeps well on those odds.

He should thank God his chief adviser just happened to be there in the bed with him. If Aline hadn't got up and locked the bedroom door, Sheila Copps would be running the place and the dollar would be worth about five cents.

Never mind the tragic consequences, imagine how embarrassing it would be if a man armed with a piece of gravel and a penknife actually managed to do away with the prime minister of Canada. In the United States, they have over two thousand Secret Service agents assigned to protect their leader, but in Canada we just hope his wife is a light sleeper.

That's what's wrong with this country. On the other hand, that's what's right with it, too.

Thank You
for Robbing Us

(First aired November 20, 1995)

If you ask the cops, they'll tell you that robberies
and muggings are down pretty well all across
Canada. They'll say the chances of becoming a
victim are less than ever before.

But of course they're only talking about being
robbed by some lowlife in a ski mask. Your
chances of being robbed by some lowlife in a
three-piece suit are running somewhere around
one hundred percent.

Look at the business pages. Every bank in
Canada is now in the process of raising its service
charges and creating new ones where they never
existed before. Now, if you're rich, they'll give you
a break. But if you're poor, well, they'll charge you
for putting your money in, for taking it out, for writing a cheque, for paying a bill, for using your card,

and for not using your card. If they could figure out a way to charge you for using the pen that's chained to the counter, they'd do it. And why? Because they only made $1.8 billion off service charges last year alone.

That's why people don't have any money in this country. The banks keep taking it, and they're not spending it. You'd think with that kind of money they could manage to keep the bank machine area a little cleaner than, say, your average public urinal.

Did He Say "Reputation"?

(First aired November 27, 1995)

Just when we're all getting used to the idea that Brian Mulroney is out of our lives, back he comes and he's worse than before. He's like the Ebola virus.

First time around he just treated us like dirt. Now he figures he's the one being treated badly and so he wants $50 million for damaging his reputation. That's what he figures it's worth, $50 million.

Yah, he deserves special treatment, all right — shock treatment. We already know that if he's found guilty, he'll be treated better than any other Canadian criminal. Being a former prime minister, he could fetch upwards of, oh, I dunno, a whole package of Player's Light in prison.

And it would be the defining Canadian moment

that we've always needed. Americans say, "Where were you when they shot JFK?" Yah, well, where were you when Irish eyes stopped smiling?

The Last Straw

(First aired December 4, 1995)

Did I miss something somewhere? Lucien Bouchard lost the referendum. Look up "loser" and there's Lucien. And even though he lost, he says there is no way Quebec will ever negotiate with Canada. Instead, he's gonna keep having referendum after referendum until he finally gets his own way.

He's like a ten-year-old having a temper tantrum in the middle of Toys 'Я Us. And instead of hauling him out and putting him in the car, Chrétien is starting to fill up the cart. Distinct culture, constitutional veto, Hot Wheels, Tonka, Nerf gun, Dinky toys, whatever it takes.

But, nope, nothing is good enough for Lucien. It's every toy in the shop or nothing. Hey, Jean, if you don't watch it, you're gonna spoil that youngster, and we're gonna have to live with it.

Lucien, you lost, you're a loser, and losers negotiate. Everyone wants Quebec to stay in Canada and sooner or later you're gonna have to take yes for an answer.

But if this bawling doesn't stop soon, next thing you know, instead of unity rallies, the rest of Canada is gonna be saying, "That's it, I'm taking off the belt," and then you'll really have something to cry about. The car gets pulled over and you'll be walking home with an arse the colour of the Maple Leaf.

Spoiled

(First aired December 18, 1995)

Now, I don't want the people of British Columbia to take this the wrong way. God love ya. You got a lot going for you. You got the beautiful mountains, great weather, you can swim in your ocean without having to freeze to death. The people I've met from there are nice enough. But, boys, oh, boys, I hate to be the one to tell you, but over the last couple of weeks, you've been starting to sound a lot like Quebec. Look, somebody had to tell you.

First you wanted a constitutional veto. You couldn't believe you weren't given the veto. Give us the veto, you said. So then they gave you the veto, and what happens? You said, I can't believe they gave us a veto! You've never been so insulted in all your lives.

And now? Now you want more or something "bad" is going to happen. Please, please, on behalf of the rest of the country, I'm begging you, stop now before it's too late. You're on a very slippery slope. Can demands for distinct society be far behind?

And, sure, you're already distinct. You've got the most stable economy in the entire country. What am I saying? You've *got* an economy. That's as distinct as you're gonna get in Canada. Where I come from, people are more worried about becoming an *extinct* society.

You think you're feeling left out? Imagine how Prince Edward Island feels! Everything the average Canadian knows about P.E.I. comes from *Road to Avonlea* and, sure, they make that in Ontario.

You got everything going for you. You're better off than most. But, please, one problem child at a time.

Tobin to the Rescue

(First aired January 15, 1996)

Clyde Wells and Brian Tobin. They're both members of the same party, they both walk upright, but the similarity ends there.

Clyde Wells is a lawyer. A lawyer's lawyer, the type of lawyer a lawyer would hire if he was going to sue a lawyer. He was premier for seven years and he never cracked a smile. The only Newfoundlander on the face of the planet with absolutely no sense of humour.

And then there's Brian. He went away to Ottawa sixteen years ago. He had to, what else was he gonna do? He was a skinny little guy with a bad moustache, the type of guy who looked like he owned the only bar within a two-hundred-mile radius. The type of guy whose dream car would have been a '77 Trans-Am, with a great big bald eagle on the bonnet. A Burt Reynolds wannabe.

But look at him now. The Turbonator, famous for firing shots across the bow of a foreign trawler. Which, let's face it, is hardly a wholly original idea in Newfoundland. Captain Canada, famous for suggesting we all fly to Montreal and tell them how much we love them. Which, let's face it, probably was his idea, come to think of it.

And now after that success on the mainland, all he had to do was say the word and Clyde's job is now his. The heir-apparent of Newfoundland and Labrador.

Now, whether he does a good job or not is yet to be seen. But for now, his greatest asset is one that all Newfoundlanders have in common: he's not Clyde Wells.

Normal Times Call for Drastic Measures

(First aired January 22, 1996)

The Ottawa–Carleton Board of Health was faced with some bad news this week. In a confidential survey, one in seven teenagers say they smoke.

Teenagers! Imagine. Apparently, they're out there now, as we speak — smoking! The most sensible, level-headed people on the planet — and they smoke.

But don't worry. The board of health has a solution. They want convenience store owners to demand I.D. of any person buying cigarettes who looks like they may be under thirty. It's the first stop on the way to the day when everyone will have to show I.D.

Simply take a convenience store, a place you shop for convenience, and turn it into the store where you have to wait in line for twenty minutes while Peter Gzowski gets his I.D. checked before he's allowed to buy his package of Rothmans Special Lights.

The board of health knows it's drastic, but the kids in the survey also said they don't think smoking is bad for them. Look, I remember getting a confidential drug survey in grade ten. Every guy in the class wrote down that we did heroin three to four times a week. Why? *Because we were teenagers!*

Most of us hadn't had a beer yet, but there was our guidance counsellor on the news making a tool of herself talking about a needle-exchange program. Now, I always assumed morons like that were destined to become and remain guidance counsellors, but no, apparently the board of health is riddled with 'em too.

There's always people out there who figure the way to solve every problem is just to create more rules. Unfortunately, a disproportionate number of them work for the government.

Voluntary Pain

(First aired January 29, 1996)

It has been said before that Lucien Bouchard is mad as a hatter. For years now, the rumour mill churned with reports that he's completely off his head and that he suffers from some sort of wonky messiah complex.

Well, now it's no longer rumour or innuendo, it's fact. The man had a pension, people gave him grief about it, and now he's gonna take that pension and give it to the State of Quebec. Nuts is an understatement.

And then there's Brian Tobin. Like Lucien, he left Ottawa with a gold-plated pension and now people are saying he should give it up too. But nobody in Newfoundland is saying it. Why? Because they know it would be a total waste of time, that's why.

Show me a Newfoundlander who would voluntarily give up fifty grand a year and I'll show you someone who is so out of touch with his people that he's not even qualified to live there, let alone lead the place.

It's just like a buddy of mine. He got fourteen GST rebates in the mail in one week. He didn't deserve the cheques. He shouldn't have got the cheques. But the important thing is, he cashed the cheques. Why? 'Cuz they were there, that's why. Who could blame him?

If we don't want politicians to have pensions until they're sixty-five, fine. But beware the politician who would give up his pension on his own. 'Cuz if they're willing to do that, they're capable of anything.

Happy Birthday, Fifty-Year-Old

(First aired February 5, 1996)

It's been in the news lately that baby boomers are turning fifty. In fact, to avoid the subject, you'd have to be a vegetable. Baby boomers turning fifty has huge sociological ramifications. Soon they won't even be called baby boomers any more, just old people.

You read the lifestyle section of the paper, it's all about baby boomers trying to look young. Read the business page, denture stocks are poised to go through the roof. Read the real estate section, homes without stairs are big gainers.

Watch the American Music Awards and the Eagles are winning awards for "Hotel California." And it sounds just as good now as it did when it was recorded a hundred years ago.

And all of a sudden every baby boomer politician out there is talking about family values. They don't care about family values. They can just smell the nursing home and they don't wanna go. The first generation to put their parents in old-age homes is starting to have second thoughts.

Of course, anyone with the misfortune to be born after the baby boom has to look forward to a lifetime of hearing about baby boomer milestones. Turning fifty will be a joke compared to turning sixty.

And the only upside to them all hitting sixty-five is that the ensuing brouhaha will be so loud we'll barely be able to hear them suck the Canada Pension Plan dry, leaving the rest of us with a lifetime of contributions and nothing to show for it.

So, Happy Birthday, baby boomers. And here's to 2046, the year they start to turn one hundred.

Warning: The Following Will Make You Nauseated

(First aired February 12, 1996)

If you watch television, they often put a warning for sensitive viewers at the top of the show. They should do the same thing with newspapers, 'cuz sometimes you're reading a paper and before you know it, you've read something so disturbing that it stays with you for weeks.

Last week, the *Ottawa Citizen* had on its front page the story of how Mike Harris orchestrated his rise to power. It went well beyond the need-to-know basis. Every time I close my eyes, there it is.

Apparently, when Mike Harris and his wife lived in North Bay, they passed the time by having friends over for dinner and afterwards they would invite them to discuss the future of Ontario over a glass of wine and a hot tub.

Imagine that: going to Mike Harris's house for dinner and he asks you to take a bath with him. It's like some sleazy seventies suburban swingers movie. Big old Mike sitting across from you, his arm around the wife, no shirt on, sweating into the tub, talking about his bid for power. Who does he think he is? Hugh Hefner?

But you got to admit, cutting welfare and putting people out on the streets would be a breeze after a soak with Mike. I guess if you want to be in the Tory loop, you gotta do your time in the tub.

The upside is that if you're a member of the Legislature and you're invited to Mike's for dinner, and he opens the door wearing a wine glass and a Speedo, you know you're in the Cabinet.

Till Death Do Us Part

(First aired February 19, 1996)

For some reason, I was under the impression that:
a) the referendum was over; and b) Pierre Trudeau
had promised to keep his mouth shut.

It's been said before that those who can't remember the past are condemned to repeat it. Unless
you're in Canada, where those who remember the
past are condemned to call press conferences
and rehash it over and over again.

That's what Trudeau does, and why not? He loves
the past. In the past, young nurses wanted to
have sex with him. Now they just want to know if
he's done his water.

And Lucien Bouchard is just as bad. It's all the
Night of the Long Knives and the Plains of
Abraham with him too. Look, French and English
Canada, like it or not, we're married. And like a
lot of marriages, it's kinda miserable, but it's a

marriage nonetheless, for better or worse. We've had the worse, now let's get on with the better.

And if we'd just accentuate the positive for a minute, it's amazing how rosy the future looks. You could say that despite it all we're still like a couple of newlyweds on our honeymoon. We are going at it every single chance we get. The spark is definitely still there and it's definitely not boring. Which by any standard is not bad for a couple that has been together for 129 years.

Chrétien the Heavy

(First aired February 26, 1996)

I hate to admit it. I know it's wrong to find joy in other people's misfortune, but I, for one, am glad the prime minister grabbed that buddy by the neck. And after watching buddy's press conference, I hope he does it again soon. In fact, just as he was accusing the prime minister of permanently staining democracy for all time, I was hoping Chrétien would pop out from behind the curtain and go for round two.

And why not? It's exciting stuff, it's good television, and everyone loves it.

Let's face it, the mook in the stupid hat sure did. For him, having the prime minister throttle ya is like winning the Lotto. Now he gets to call press conferences and the press actually shows up.

The White House even issued a statement saying that it would never happen in America. Now, granted, the bullet that's still lodged in Ronald Reagan's ass was not available for comment. But still, it's big news and everyone came out a winner: the choker, the chokee, and the lowly TV viewer. Overall, it was the best Flag Day ever. Next year, I might even go.

National Unrest

(First aired March 4, 1996)

Obviously, there's a lot of Canadians out there who are not happy. Everywhere you look, east, west, north, south, there they are, waving signs shouting "Down with This One," "Up with That One," "Out with X," "In with Y."

Problem is, it doesn't work any more. It's gotten to the point where you can't even tell if buddy with the sign is an actual protester or if he's selling RRSPs for the Bank of Montreal.

And strikes. Premiers used to be afraid of thousands of people marching off the job in protest. Now, none of them could be bothered. The first thing Mike Harris said when the crowd in Ontario went on strike was, "Good! The people will save millions!" What people?, I ask. The people on the picket line are people, they're not saving money. And the people who used to sell stuff to the people on the picket line are people, and they're not saving money. But the person who leads the people is the premier, and he figures ignoring the people is fiscally responsible.

If the public service unions in this country want to get attention, they should do exactly the opposite of what they're doing in Ontario. Stay at work, cash their cheques, then go out on the lawn and cut up their credit cards. Over a million and a half credit cards snipped up in a pile. Then let the banks call the premiers. Unlike the unions, that's a call they'll take.

Good Fences

(First aired March 11, 1996)

There's a lot of arguments out there for and against trade with Cuba. But the best one for increasing it so far is that the United States wants us to stop.

In their self-appointed overzealous mission as defenders of freedom, they have finally reached the point where they've decided that sovereign nations like Canada are only free to do what America tells them to do.

Yah, if the United States was a thirty-five-year-old male, he'd be in a mental hospital — for his sake, for our sake, and for the sake of the whole neighbourhood. And the diagnosis? Below-average intelligence, suffers from delusions of grandeur, medicate heavily.

Unfortunately, America is too big to get the restraints on and they're not in a very good mood.

Of course they're not. If I looked that stupid I'd be pissed off too.

America stopped trade with Cuba to teach them a lesson in 1961. And now, thirty-five years later, Cuba's trading with everyone else to teach America a lesson. Businesses are springing up left, right, and centre and not one of them is American. Castro the Commie is becoming Castro the Capitalist. He's open for business and Canadians have every right to be there. Because, hey, Canada's a free country, and freedom's not just another word for doing what America tells ya.

Sad Bankers

(First aired March 18, 1996)

I feel bad, I feel really bad. I didn't know this, but banks are people, too. They have feelings. They have their ups and their downs. They have ambitions and broken dreams. And they have pain, they said so themselves.

The chairman of the Royal Bank announced that they made a profit of $356 million in ninety days. But, you know, they're not happy. No, they're sad, sad because they want broader powers and the government won't give them to them. What a mean government!

The banks are tired of just taking people's money. They want to be able to sell life insurance and lease cars and small appliances. They want to put car dealers out of work, insurance salesmen on the dole, and the poor suckers who sell stereos out on the street. But the government won't let them. That's the source of their pain.

It's time to lay off the bank bashing. And just for a minute, let's put ourselves in their shoes. Try to put ourselves inside the mind of a bunch of self-centred whiny millionaires who aren't happy unless their gums are flapping and it's all about them and how they deserve more and nobody likes them and they'll never be happy. Try to do it and you will see how sad they are, really, really sad.

The View from
the Cheap Seats

(First aired March 25, 1996)

I went to Ottawa recently and for the first time in
my life I sat up in the spectators' gallery and
watched our nation's elected leaders go about the
business of running the country.

It was one of the weirdest things I have ever
done. I go in there about half an hour before
Question Period, and there's only five people in
the whole House. There's three Liberal back-
benchers, one Bloc, and over on the Reform
side, Deborah Grey. She's standing up all alone
in the middle of this huge empty room, screaming to beat the band, arms going, fingers point-
ing at the prime minister — who wasn't there —
demanding immediate answers to questions
that nobody could hear. She was like something
out of *One Flew Over the Cuckoo's Nest*. Except
you knew no matter how many times the evil

nurse gave her shock treatment, she would never shut up.

And then the bell rang. And, boom, the place is blocked for Question Period. You just don't got the real feel of Question Period on TV. You've really got to be there. Either that, or close your eyes and imagine your grade eight class with a substitute teacher. They're booing, hissing, yelling, screaming, throwing paper balls, ignoring the Speaker.

And then, out of the blue, one MP called another MP a liar. Well, the place went up. Because apparently the worst thing you can do in the House of Commons is call someone a liar. If you call someone a liar, and you don't apologize, you're kicked out of the House. Which is ironic, seeing as that's how most of them get in there in the first place. But if you're an MP you can lie all you want and nobody will call you a liar, because that would be the truth, and the truth is not allowed when it comes to lying, because in the House there are no liars. Just like in the big house, there are no guilty men.

The Great Flag Robbery

(First aired September 30, 1996)

Look, Ma, free flag. Compliments of Sheila Copps. Because Sheila Copps is desperately concerned about Canadian unity. And Sheila is one of those rare politicians: a politician who can look past the needs of the sick, the poor, and the elderly and see the real Canadian victims out there. The people who suffer in silence, the people who have a flagpole but no flag. Often, it's not even their fault. They didn't want the pole: "It came with the cottage, the damn thing's set in concrete."

But when Sheila saw all of these people's poles standing straight up, buck naked in the wind, she had a dream. A dream where she would spend seven million tax dollars and give away a million flags. But her dream was a fantasy. Because you can't buy a million flags for seven million bucks. And then the dream became a nightmare and before we knew it she had to spend 23 million tax dollars sending idiots like me a flag.

And before we could say, "No, no, stop, take the flags back," she had another dream. This time she had a dream to start a whole new government department called the Heritage Information Office. And once again the dream became a reality and $20 million later, the office is open and nobody knows what they do because there is no information on what the Information Office does. Oh, she's dreaming all right. She thinks she's Ivana Trump with a Gold Card.

Sheila, please, if you have any more dreams of Canadian unity, the country is gonna have to be sold off for parts. For the love of God and country, stop dreaming. Wake up!

Can a Bank Change?

(First aired October 14, 1996)

For over a year now, the Bank of Montreal has been running one of the most bizarre and irritating ad campaigns in the history of television.

For some reason, lost on me, it makes sense for a bank to promote itself by showing us endless pictures of people that a bank wouldn't cross the road to spit on, let alone lend money to. And these poor, confused, worried people always hold up signs and ask the same question: Can a bank change?

And just when we thought the suspense would kill us or we'd kill ourselves if we had to watch it one more time, they've changed. They've lost the protester-with-a-sign look and ordered up a whack of beautiful, healthy, smiling children running through golden fields of wheat singing Bob Dylan's "The Times They Are A-Changin'."

There's change for ya. What used to be an anthem

against people like the bank is now a jingle for the bank. And it's a nice jingle, too. If you listen carefully, you can actually hear the sound of Woody Guthrie spinning in his grave.

I know all the banks are courting baby boomers, but what are they gonna do next? Put every teller in a tie-dyed tank top? Give every tenth customer a brain toke? Dig up John Lennon and give him a sign? Why not? They bought Bob Dylan, gave him a quarter, and made him dance.

Can a bank change? I dunno, but they can't sink much lower, I know that.

Careers

(First aired October 21, 1996)

If you walk around any city in this country you'll get hit up for loose change. And now all across Canada, towns are following the city of Ottawa's lead. Because in Ottawa they've made it illegal to ask for money!

Ottawanians are very practical, and they realize that people are homeless because they made a career choice. They went to career day, came home, and said, "Mom, forget the BA in poli-sci at Carleton, I'm gonna be homeless."

Being homeless pays three dollars a day, you get beaten up a lot, and you have nowhere to sleep at night. But now you can't do it anymore. So if you're homeless in Ottawa, you have two choices. Become a lobbyist or stay homeless. Which means you're not only miserable, you're also a criminal because you ask people for money.

I know some people are saying, "It would be fine if the homeless spent the money on food but they spend it on alcohol." Well, of course they do. If I ended up walking the streets of Canada talking to parking meters all day, I'd want a drink, too.

But what can we do? Treatment? Sure, coun-selling works, but, hey, we're all cutting back, right? They'll just have to tighten their belts like anyone else. Now, mind you, they have no belts. So have the cops pick 'em up, charge 'em, got them a lawyer, send them to court, appear before a judge, find them guilty, and fine them fifty bucks. If they don't have their chequebook on them, send them to jail for a week and then back out on the street.

They say you can't legislate against stupidity. Well, now I know why: because our legislators would be the ones doing all the hard time — just like the homeless.

Empty Preston

(First aired October 28, 1996)

Starting a political party in Canada is not easy. It's way up there with starting a major religion. But Preston Manning, he did the work, he beat the odds, and for that he deserves a lot of credit. He built it and they came.

Overnight the Reform Party became like the Catholic faith of the political set. They never compromised, they passed the plate at every meeting, and they had an infallible leader with a flair for fashion — the king of the deficit reduction. And the more he preached about cutting the deficit, the more they came, and soon he had visions of being the king of Parliament Hill.

But unfortunately, just like with the Catholics, all the other parties moved in and borrowed all the best policies, leaving all the questionable parts behind. The Liberals borrowed so heavily from Reform that Canadians actually believe they have the deficit under control, problem solved.

And where does that leave Preston? Nowhere! That's where. He's desperate. The poor guy is out there now, running around, waving a document called "Fresh Start." A Reform Party document that calls for increased — not decreased, increased — spending on health care and education. A great idea, but, please, Preston, coming from you, it's blasphemy. That's like the pope coming out of surgery and saying, "Strap on a condom, boys, I changed my mind."

I feel bad for the man, I really do. You know, I think he loved that deficit like it was his very own. But being reduced to telling people that he'll be the saviour of the social safety net. It's sad, really. It's worse than the emperor has no clothes; it's the emperor has no ideas.

Democracy, American-Style

(First aired November 4, 1996)

Within hours the citizens of America, the strongest nation on Earth, are going to wake up and go to the polls. It will be the greatest display of democracy on the face of the planet. Yet sixty percent of Americans couldn't give a rat's ass about voting. They'd just as soon see Porky Pig in the White House. They'll be lucky if they get fifty percent of the people off the couch and into the polling booth.

Why? Because this election has been so boring! If I was an American, I'd be suicidal. And why? Ethics! All of a sudden, Bill Clinton and Bob Dole got it into their heads that just being politicians wasn't good enough. They wanted to appear ethical. They didn't want people to think they were running negative campaigns. They didn't want to look dirty.

Don't they realize? Politics is like the movies. Without the dirty parts, it's over. It might have a happy ending, but nobody is going to watch. Even worse, nobody is going to care.

Hopefully, this is a trend that will not move north of the border. I like our way better. Canadians are much more practical. We know what politicians are: egomaniacs with a genetic predisposition for public speaking. That's it. As far as ethics go, if they knew right from wrong, they wouldn't be running for office in the first place.

The Paper It's Written On

(First aired November 8, 1996)

When Jean Chrétien was running for the big job he made a lot of promises. He promised a Chevrolet government, no secrets, and the strictest ethics guidelines in the history of Canada. And now, four years later turns out the reason why it's not against the rules for a minister to charge a fur coat on a Chevrolet government credit card is because the ethics guidelines don't even exist!

There's something smelly on Parliament Hill and it's not coming from the pigeons. The prime minister had said over and over that the rules exist but they are confidential. Now the ethics commissioner says they don't exist. So Chrétien is lying, but that's okay because he's not breaking any rules, because they're not written down.

Maybe they did exist. Maybe they lost them.

Maybe the dog peed on them. Who knows? Can a minister steal? Who's to say? Can he hire a hooker and fly to Fiji? Depends — was it on business? This is like Moses coming down from the Mount and saying, "You shall not covet your neighbour's wife, but me, on the other hand, I operate off a much stricter set of tablets." Then he goes off, sleeps with your wife, and gets caught with his pants down. Unfortunately for Jean, getting caught with your pants down in this day and age is nothing compared to getting caught lying about how you can't lie because you have a set of rules that say you can't when you don't.

If I were you, Jean, I'd start scribbling.

Impressions
of Washington

(First aired November 11, 1996)

When you walk around Washington, D.C., you can't help but be in total awe of the place. It's the epicentre of the last great superpower left standing, and, boy, do they know it. But Canadians should feel proud of them, happy for them. Because America is our neighbour, our ally, our trading partner, and our friend.

Still, sometimes you'd like to give them such a smack! But we can't. If we tried, let's face it, they would kill us. And therein lies the problem. Pierre Trudeau said it was a lot like a relationship between an elephant and a mouse. Brian Mulroney, to give him the benefit of the doubt, felt that Canada could influence America more from the inside. Therefore, he devoted most of his public life trying to get the mouse up inside the elephant. And, let's face it, that's a period in our country's history we'd all like to forget.

So what are we gonna do? Well, for starters, we have to think differently. We have to erase this whole elephant/mouse analogy from our minds. America is *not* an elephant. For one thing, elephants never forget, whereas Americans don't really know much to begin with. Ninety percent of them can't pick out their home town on an unmarked map. We're bigger than they are and we're on top. If we were in prison, they'd be our bitch. Our role is to remind them of the little things like that, over and over and over again. And if they get mad with us, we'll just have to take our name off the map and feel safe in knowing that they will never find us.

Good News?

(First aired November 18, 1996)

In my lifetime there has only been bad news. Bad news about the country, the debt, the future, the works. I figured that's just the way it worked: every morning you'd wake up, read your paper, get a smack in the head, and go about your day.

But the good thing about all bad news was that it meant we were all in the same boat. It was a sinking boat, but, hey, we were united, all for one, one for all. But now, all of a sudden, the papers are filled with good news. Great news. Except for some odd reason it's only about the crowd who were in first class. Who somehow managed to sneak a few life rafts on board and not tell anyone they were there.

The good news is that if you're in the market for a dream home, interest rates are in the toilet. The time to borrow money from the bank is *now*. Problem is, Canadians aren't in the market for a dream home; they're in the market for snow tires, and the interest rate on the Canadian Tire card is still somewhere short of loan sharking.

The good news is that continuous downsizing has meant foreign investors have a renewed confidence in Canada. Well, that's good, except it's got Canadians so freaked out they're afraid to buy anything that's not edible.

Don't get me wrong. It's not that people aren't grateful that the stock market just hit a new high. It's just that so did the unemployment rate. And the sight of the champagne corks popping on the life rafts doesn't really help when you're still treading water.

Good Work—
If Someone Else
Will Do It

(First aired November 25, 1996)

Canadians by and large are a decent lot, and when we get bombarded with images like those coming out of Zaire, we respond. We want to help in any way we can. We agree, yes, we should send in Canada's peacekeepers. That's what they're there for.

But when it comes right down to it, that's basically it. After that we make plans for supper. Because most Canadians are like me: if asked, I wouldn't go. I mean, I'd like to, but I couldn't. I grew up in a bungalow. I have plans for Christmas, I can't just drop everything and fly halfway around the world and plunk myself down in the middle of two warring factions.

Most of us freak out when the boss tells us to work late. Imagine getting the call to drop everything, get on a plane, you're going to the worst place on Earth — for Canada. And don't worry, you'll still get paid crap. Oh, yeah, if they go, a lot of our peacekeepers will make, including danger pay, twenty grand a year before taxes.

If they do a good job, we all get the credit. And if a few of them screw up, they all take the blame. Not a bad deal for the 25 million Canadians who are gonna stay here. But maybe, just maybe the ones who might be going deserve a bit of a raise.

Bouchard
the Survivor

(First aired December 2, 1996)

I got sucked in last week. There was speculation that Lucien Bouchard might be forced to resign and I actually believed it.

I figured, why not? His own party turned on him at their convention, they embarrassed him in public, and he's probably tired. I figured if I was Lucien Bouchard, I'd probably jump off a building. But, no, he survived, because Lucien Bouchard is like no other politician. He's like the political equivalent of a German cockroach. A nuclear war couldn't end his career.

As we all know, Lucien has had to overcome some pretty traumatic obstacles in the past. It's nothing to make light of, but very few people have ever survived the effects of being in Brian Mulroney's cabinet. Lucien did. When all his buddies were

114

either going up on charges or going down in defeat, he formed his very own party and became Leader of the Opposition.

And when the separatists lost the referendum and the Opposition were left looking like a bunch of dummies, he high-tailed it out of Ottawa and became premier of Quebec. And the members of the PQ couldn't get rid of him if they tried. They could chew him up and spit him out in eight pieces and, I swear to God, all eight pieces would stand up, walk away, and start their own party before the week was out.

No, Bouchard will survive. But whether the PQ will or not, that's up for debate.

In Praise of
Older Tories

(First aired December 9, 1996)

Christmas is coming, the malls are packed, people are frantic. But the question remains: What do you get the country that has everything?

Well, I hate to admit it, I'm afraid that if I even say it the ground will open up and swallow me whole, but what this country needs is Tories. Old-fashioned, bull-headed, know-it-all Canadian Tories. A great big whack of them. Just to sit across from the Liberals and rattle their cage. Because if we don't, the Liberals' heads are gonna explode.

As it stands now, they already giggle themselves sick on the way into Question Period every day. There is no national Opposition. Reformers are dropping like flies. And the Bloc can't even find anyone willing to suffer the humiliation of being their leader.

Granted, four years ago the entire country sent every Tory in Canada off to bed without their supper. We took 'em aside, told them everything was awful, it was all your fault and to go to your room and stay there until you apologize. But maybe the time has come to give 'em a bite to eat and let 'em out for a while. They've learned their lesson and they're hungry.

I'm not saying we give them the keys to the house — no, no, no — we just let 'em babysit the Liberals for a while. And if they do a good job, maybe we'll take it from there.

Chrétien's Town Hall Defeat

(First aired December 31, 1996)

There's an election coming, you can smell it in the air. Either that, or I stepped in something. Nope. It's an election, all right, and my guess is the Liberals are hoping we'll drink so much this New Year's that we'll forget the last month of 1996 altogether. Because, ya know, they have to be asking themselves: How will history judge Jean Chrétien's 1996?

Well, let's see. He went off on a few trips. He almost lost the country in a referendum. And he took a few beatings in the House of Commons. But the Liberals know the Opposition can say whatever they want about the prime minister, nobody cares. But when a normal Canadian fires off a few shots it can be fatal.

Everyone remembers the little old lady who

called Brian Mulroney a liar and everyone is going to remember the waitress from Montreal who stood up to Jean Chrétien and said the very same thing. Hey, Jean, I used to work in a restaurant, I'll let you in on a little secret: never piss off the waitress. She can ruin your night. And by the looks of the polls, this one might have ruined his entire year.

If I was the prime minister of this country and I was facing an election, I'd have one New Year's resolution: to stay the hell away from Canadians. And barring that, leave better tips.

Ontari-ari-ari-o

(First aired January 20, 1997)

Has anyone else noticed that every time the government of Ontario makes an announcement, it sounds less and less like government policy and more and more like a Leon's Furniture ad?

Like last week. Last week wasn't just any old week, last week was "Mega Week." You know, Mega Week, it happens just after the "Boxing Day Don't-Pay-a-Cent Event." Everything must be cut! Everything must go! And the deals? The minister of education has said that, thanks to him, the kids are gonna get a better education with less money.

Wow! "More for Less," that sounds great. Just like "No Down Payment, No Payment 'Til Next Year" sounds great — if you're an idiot.

Am I the only person who finds it just a little odd that Ontario's minister of education dropped out of high school? He should be minister in charge of cutting meat, not cutting education.

"More for Less" might convince people to buy a bedroom set, but when it comes to education, "More for Less" really means "Save Now, Pay Big Later."

Canada's
Manifest Destiny

(First aired January 27, 1997)

Lloyd Axworthy, Canada's last true liberal, headed to Cuba last week. And good for him. It's supposed to be very nice this time of year. Actually, I'm glad he went, because the thought of a Canadian cabinet minister lunching with Fidel Castro had the Americans so mad, they didn't know whether to swallow or spit.

Now, Lloyd says he only talked to Fidel about increasing trade and human rights. I say, do it one better. I say, we take a page from Lucien Bouchard's book and talk about sovereignty-association, not between Canada and Quebec, but between Canada and Cuba. We could call it "Canuba."

When you think about it, "Canuba" sounds more Canadian than "Canada." Now, granted, there's a few bugs to work out. Like we're the True North Strong and Free, and they're neither. But, c'mon, Canadians love a beach. And we can offer a lot to Cuba.

We're already their largest trading partner. We've got a strong currency, we're in NAFTA, and we still believe in universal health care and education. And the best thing is that on the pissing-off-America scale, this would be a ten. And when they complained, we could say, "Ahhh, shut up, we've got you surrounded!"

Teflon Jean

(First aired February 3, 1997)

For the last three and a half years Jean Chrétien has been the Teflon prime minister. No matter what he did, nothing stuck, and there was no mess to clean up. But now, all of a sudden, the party's popularity is in the toilet and Chrétien's popularity is actually somewhere below that. And apparently, he's in shock.

Obviously this is a man who doesn't cook his own breakfast because, when it comes to Teflon, everyone knows it only lasts three or four years and then all it takes is one little scratch. Next thing you know, your eggs are stuck to the pan. And the more you go at it, the bigger the scratch, and all of a sudden your no-stick pan is swallowing omelettes and it's not even fit for the cottage.

And that's kinda where the Liberals are right now. And to stop us from throwing the whole works out, they've come up with a really good plan. They're going to drop this whole cutting-the-deficit thing and campaign on the promise of jobs, jobs, jobs. Which begs the question: how stupid does Jean Chrétien think we are? I mean, he's gonna get re-elected anyway, but does he have to go around telling us he's going to do all the things he said he'd do in the first place, but decided not to do once he got elected? The Liberals should be honest. Instead of jobs, jobs, jobs, they should tell the truth: vote Liberal, the lesser of the other two evils. Well, maybe three — don't count out the Tories yet.

Power is Fleeting

(First aired February 10, 1997)

Now normally, under most circumstances, I would never say this about the prime minister, but as it stands right here and now, I think that Jean Chrétien is actually the most powerful man in Canada.

In Ottawa, on Bay Street, everyone wants to know the same thing: when is he gonna call the election? Spring or fall? He's the only one who knows and he's not telling. Although, if you think about it, there's only one logical answer: June. Because Jean Chrétien may be the prime minister but he's still a bayman — a regular old grew-up-in-a-small-Canadian-town kind of guy. And come July, Chrétien, like every other Canadian, given a choice, would rather go up to his cabin, put on his track pants, stop shavin', and fool around with the lawnmower for two months. Either that or play golf.

If it's not June, he's gonna have to spend July and August schlepping his way across Canada talking to average Canadians, who, let's face it, don't wanna be talking to him, because they want to be somewhere else wearing track pants, not shaving, and pouring beer on the barbecue.

Because of this dilemma, and because information is power, that makes Jean Chrétien the most powerful man in Canada. And that's also why he's not telling anyone. Because the minute he opens his mouth, he goes back to being just like the rest of us: just another Canadian worried about losing his job.

The PM-in-Waiting Can Wait

(First aired February 24, 1997)

Paul Martin's budget made one thing positively clear: Liberals care about young people. They're a national priority! He said so himself. In the middle of the budget speech, he just blurted it out. He said that "the young are our most precious natural resource."

And the week before that, he put his money where his mouth is. He revamped the entire Canada Pension Plan. If you retired in 1995, you'll end up getting seven times the amount of money you paid in. And if you're under twenty-five, you're gonna pay in twice as much as they did and get less money.

Well, on behalf of the youth of Canada, Mr. Martin, let me be the first to thank you, ya big tool. What are we supposed to do with that information?

Should we start eating cat food now to get used to the taste? Or should we wait another twenty years for the baby boomers to belly up to the trough and see what happens then? Paul Martin is counting on two things: that people under twenty-five don't vote and that they don't pay attention to pensions.

For his sake, he better hope the trend continues. Otherwise, come election day, they mightn't be so eager to respect their elders. Especially their Liberal ones.

Hello, Dolly!

(First aired March 3, 1997)

When you're watching the news, it's very important to start at the top of a story. Don't pick it up
halfway through. Last week, I flick on the news
and there's this Scottish guy telling Peter
Mansbridge that he's done it with a sheep, he's
hoping to do it with a cow, and with luck, he'll get
to do it with a pig — but he drew the line at
humans!

Now, I'm already prepared at this point to be dis-
turbed, but cloning sheep? No, no, no! Scotland
has just given us the new worst thing that can
be done to a sheep. It's the *Boys from Brazil*
meets *Animal Farm*.

Now, a recent poll said that most people are
against cloning animals, but at the same time
they wouldn't mind if they found out science had
gone ahead and cloned John Lennon. Which, sure,
would be great, but the problem is, they've only

done it with female sheep, so the best that modern science could offer would be Yoko Ono.

Why don't we just quit while we're ahead? There's all sorts of things that we know we are capable of that we just don't do. Like putting tinfoil in the microwave or voting Reform east of Toronto. And when it comes to sheep, I say, let the age-old adage apply: just don't do it!

Toronto the Better

(First aired March 10, 1997)

I don't get to go to Toronto that often. But I was there last week. And I gotta tell you, after just one weekend, when I flew out last Monday, I felt like I was on the last flight out before the Fall of Saigon.

The provincial government was telling the people of Toronto that they didn't care how they voted on the megacity, they were going to ignore them. And the City of Toronto was telling business owners they didn't care how they felt about running their own bars and restaurants, they were going to ignore them. No smoking anywhere, in any restaurant ever, no matter what the owners want.

No wonder Torontonians are in such a bad mood all the time — every level of government is constantly ignoring them. I had no idea. I actually feel bad for them. They've lost some pretty important battles.

This is a country where, if you vote on something, it's supposed to count. And if your idea of a classy restaurant is a place that sells raw meat on a stick and the only drink is whisky, and if you smoke during dinner you get a free table dance, well, so be it. You can open that restaurant, run it the way you want, then you get to retire rich. That's what living in a free country is all about.

Toronto is not only like no other city in Canada, it's not even like Canada any more.

Jobs, Jobs, Jobs ... in the Philippines

(First aired March 17, 1997)

The latest unemployment figures are in and all the economists are saying the same thing: when it comes to job creating, the economy is stalled. Although the finance minister disagrees with the term "stalled." And he's right. When you see a '73 Datsun B 210 with no doors and the engine up on blocks, do you say, "Look, that car is stalled"? No! You say, "Look, that car is not working." And you know that someone promised to fix that four years ago.

Now, sure, we could blame the finance minister, but that would be too easy. Besides, the finance minister blames the private sector.

Oh, yeah, Paul Martin said he's worried because the private sector refuses to create entry-level jobs for young people. And he *should* be worried.

Take that boat, for example, that belongs to Canada Steamship Lines, one of the biggest shipping companies in Canada. They're building two more ships this year to sail the Seven Seas. Now, if I was a young Canadian with no job, why couldn't I just go aboard and apply for an entry-level job on one of their brand-new ships?

I'll tell you why: because Canada Steamship Lines is owned by Paul Martin. Blind trusts and all, it's still *his* company. And they're going to register their new ships in Bermuda and hire people in the Philippines, to save money.

So I'm not surprised Paul Martin is worried about the young people. I'm just surprised that he sleeps at night.

Fun with Candidates

(First aired March 24, 1997)

Well, the word is we're all going to the polls in June. Now, granted, most Canadians would rather have a root canal. But if you have the right attitude you'll know this is the only time that the average citizen can actually benefit from the democratic process. Because it's the only time politicians suddenly want something from you. And it's your democratic responsibility to make 'em work for it.

When a candidate knocks on the door, get them to do something for you. "Oh, yeah, I'm thinking of voting Tory, now could you help me move these boxes down into the basement?" They'll do it. And if you have to plan your kid's birthday party, call up the bouncing yogis, tell 'em you're a supporter, get 'em over and make 'em bounce up and down on the deck and entertain the kids. Better than a pony.

And if you're a senior citizen, all of your

transportation problems are solved. Call the Liberals, tell them you want a ride downtown and, if you don't get it, none of the seniors in your shallow-water fitness class will be voting Liberal this year. They'll send a minivan just like that.

Spring cleaning? Pick a party, tell 'em they can put a sign in your yard as long as they rake up the lawn. After they do that, you can take down the sign and use it to start the barbecue.

Other than that, just sit back and watch all the leaders march around every night on the news in a succession of stupid hats, doing the macarena and trying to act like one of the people. Then come election day, vote the way you always do — or mark "None of the above."

36th Parliament:
Bring on the Crazies

(First aired September 22, 1997)

Here we go again. The thirty-sixth Parliament of Canada. We've got five official parties, a brand-new Parliament, a new Opposition, a new cabinet, an old prime minister, and John Nunziata. What more could you want?

Chrétien's still the boss, sure, but this time he's got to watch his back. Let's face it, he hasn't been making a lot of sense lately, and Paul Martin is running around like Michael Corleone.

And the Reform Party? Well, who would have thought, eh? The Official Opposition! All those years we said they were just a bunch of crackpots who'd never have any power. Turns out we were only half right. And the Tories? Huge gains, all because of Jean Charest . . . keep it up. You could form a government in about five hundred years.

And the NDP are finally back on the map, and thank God, because if you can't laugh, what's the point?

But the best part about having a new Parliament is the new members. This time there are sixty-two of them. And the great thing is that nobody knows where the crazies are lurking. But they're out there. They always are. They're up there now, ready to walk up to a microphone and reveal to the world that lunatics often end up in Parliament. And we'll be waiting for them.

Carney for President

(First aired October 6, 1997)

If there is a God in heaven, there has to be a special place in hell for former Tory cabinet ministers. What is wrong with these people? They got elected, became cabinet ministers, stuck around long enough to get the big pension, and now they seem to be living out the rest of their lives trying to destroy the country, one by one.

Just when it was starting to look like Lucien Bouchard was losing support for Quebec separation, along comes Tory senator Pat Carney saying that British Columbia should separate. And why? Because Canada opened fire on Spanish fishing boats on the East Coast and they won't do the same on the West Coast. Except, of course, it's not just a few Spaniards in a rusty trawler causing trouble on the West Coast. It's a whole bunch of Americans.

Well, Pat, you've got a point. Off you go, separate.

Change your name to the Country of British Columbia and open fire on the United States. Good plan. You'd have your name changed to Greater Seattle before you could cash your last Senate cheque.

And speaking of the Senate, will the Country of British Columbia have one? And will Tory hasbeens be appointed to sit around and do nothing except cash their cheques? I doubt it. If I were you, Pat, I'd do what senators do best — keep a low profile. Either that or put your money where your mouth is and take the first step towards independence — separate yourself from the Senate.

Our Real Expensive Real Estate

(First aired October 13, 1997)

When you walk around the grounds of Rideau Hall, Canada's official residence for the Queen or her reasonable facsimile, the governor general, you can't help but be impressed. This is an expensive piece of real estate. We're talking seventy-nine acres in the middle of Ottawa. And this is not the only one, either. Oh, no, the Queen of England has official residences from one end of this country to the other. And I don't know if you noticed this, but the Queen doesn't really come over here that much. Which makes me wonder, why are we paying for all this? I mean, the lights are on. She's not home.

Actually, that's the problem. She's at home in England, in another country, which raises the question, Why is a woman in England the head of the government here in Canada? As the rules are now, if the prime minister wants to call an election, he's got to get up tomorrow morning, come on over to Rideau Hall, knock on that door and ask the Queen's representative for permission. I don't think so. If I was the prime minister I'd come over, all right. I'd come over and tell the whole lot of them they had to be out of the house by the end of the month. We're not British people any more, we're Canadian. Let's act like it. Let's get the Queen off our money and turn this place into a big park.

Alexa on Top

(First aired November 20, 1997)

Heading into the last election, the left wing were about this close to joining the right whale on Canada's endangered-species list. But the NDP beat the odds. They multiplied, they prospered, they sent twenty-one members of Parliament to Ottawa. Problem is, they made it to the dance, they just can't hear the band. So far, the only thing they have done of any note was join the Reform Party in walking out of the House. Sure, it made the news. But it also made Alexa McDonough look like Preston Manning's little sister, tagging along when he went outdoors. The streetlights came on. Haven't heard from her since.

But now the word is the NDP have a plan that will put the spotlight firmly on the cheap seats in Parliament. They are going to table legislation that would lower the voting age in Canada to sixteen. Grade ten. Which is a very smart move for the NDP. Really smart. The type of move you'd expect from a tobacco company. I should know, because I have a confession to make. When I was sixteen I was a member of the NDP. I kept the card in my wallet right next to the licence for my motorcycle, which, when I was sixteen, I used to drive really fast without a helmet. Luckily, I never had an accident and hit my head. If I had, who knows . . . I could still be a member of the NDP today.

Ice Storm '98

(First aired January 19, 1998)

It's been said that politics makes strange bed-fellows. Well, that might be true but nothing compares to the strange sleeping arrangements created by natural disasters. Who would've guessed that twelve thousand members of the Canadian military could descend on Quebec, be given special powers to arrest people on the street, and it would all have the blessing of Lucien Bouchard.

But it happened. The largest mobilization of Canadian forces in peacetime responding to the largest ice storm in Canadian history.

Once again, Canadian men and women, getting out of bed, flying to the exact place where nobody wants to go, not getting any Aeroplan points, working twenty-hour days in awful conditions, getting no overtime, doing everything in their power to help people they've never met, just because that's what they do.

Which, I guess, is why we've been laying them off hand over fist since the early nineties; a third of them are gone so far. And really who needs them? It's not like we're a great big northern country where every time you turn around there are massive floods, forest fires or ice storms or anything. And besides, when these things do happen, we can always call in the reserves. They'll show up and risk their lives, saving ours. Now can you put a price on that type of service?

Well, the federal government can . . . forty-six dollars and sixty-eight cents a day. Before taxes. About twenty-nine bucks take home.

Yes, it's quite a country we live in. It's a pretty good deal. Well, for those of us who aren't in the armed forces, anyway.

To Gouge or Not to Gouge?

(First aired January 26, 1998)

Twenty million dollars. That's what they're spending. The big babies. Twenty million dollars. The Canadian Bankers' Association is spending twenty million dollars in an effort to convince average Canadians to stop hating them.

You know, as an average Canadian, just knowing that makes me hate them twenty million times more than I did before. And, even though I'm not that good at numbers, I'm pretty sure that's a lot.

What I find amazing is that they would even try to get us to like them. They might as well get together and decide to turn water into wine. They'd have about the same chance.

So please, let me as an average Canadian, say to the Canadian Bankers' Association, just this once:

when you make seven and a half billion dollars in twelve months off average Canadians, average Canadians aren't going to like you that much. You can spend twenty million dollars. You can spend two hundred million dollars. You can sponsor the Special Olympics until your head falls off . . . it doesn't matter. As long as you keep charging people eighty-five cents to write a cheque, a buck thirty to pay a bill, or fifty cents to use one machine, and a dollar eighty-five to use another, then we're not going to like you. And not only that, we're going to like not liking you.

It's very simple. You've got two choices: keep gouging people, or stop gouging people. That's the seven and a half billion dollar question—and I bet we all know the answer.

Clinton's Dick

(First aired February 2, 1998)

Every now and then, like most Canadians, it occurs to me that it would be great if the United States of America had a great big switch. You could just reach out and flick 'em off and they'd just disappear. I'm not fanatical about it like some people, but it does cross my mind, like, say, about six or seven times a day. But the past week, its been pretty well consistent.

Is it really necessary to get up at 8:00 Saturday morning, pick up the paper and read about the exact dimensions of the president's parts? No, but we all did it, 'cuz there's no switch. Apparently it's the circumference of a quarter . . . and I know . . . without even thinking, you reached into your pocket . . . pulled out a quarter . . . looked at it . . . like you've never seen a quarter before.

See, I like our system better. Sure, we have politicians who lie, cheat, and steal and end up in prison and all that . . . but what we don't have are politicians who have sex scandals. We assume they're having sex. There is evidence to that effect . . . the Reform Party is still growing . . . but we just don't care.

Maybe Chrétien has a thing for pages. Maybe Preston Manning has a thing for stewardesses. Maybe, God forbid, Alexa McDonough's got a thing for old Tories. And if they do . . . who cares? We don't. We're too Canadian. It's a northern thing. What goes on inside the snowsuit, stays inside the snowsuit.

In Canada, sex and politics don't mix. We figure politicians have a country to run. And we've got better things to do than sit around and stare at nickles and dimes all day.

Smart Bombs

(First aired March 2, 1998)

You walk around Washington, D.C., you keep your ears open, talk to a few cab drivers, a few people on the street, and I tell ya, now that Desert Storm Part Two has been postponed, there's a feeling in the air that is hard to describe. I hate to call it relief . . . 'cuz it's not relief . . . it's more like their favourite TV show has been cancelled, before it even began.

Boy, they were really looking forward to spending a few days on the couch, drinking beer and watching a few smart bombs blow up on CNN. 'Cuz as far as this crowd is concerned, when it comes to inventions, the smart bomb is up there with the polio vaccine. But a word of advice if you're planning on visiting America soon . . . don't bring up the fact that the smart bombs were never really that smart in the first place. They don't like that. And don't talk about how smart food is called smart food, but it's really just old popcorn covered in cheese. They really don't like that. And don't call them learning disabled bombs, either . . . for some reason they take that personally.

In fact, it's best if you don't say anything at all, because man, are they pumped! They are ready to go . . . they wanna blow off some steam. America is like that big dumb guy at the dance at 3:00 in the morning . . . the lights just came on, the girls have gone home, so he's got no other choice. He's got to go out in the parking lot, close one eye . . . look for the smallest guy he can find and punch him really hard in the head.

So my advice to the entire planet: everyone lie low for a while . . . 'cuz they're really mad . . . and unfortunately, we're all out in the parking lot.

Charest's
Dilemma

(First aired March 9, 1998)

Is there anyone there who would like to trade
place with Jean Charest? 'Cuz for a guy with such
a high profile, and a lot of options, his life sucks.

There he is, the leader of the federal Tories and
the only people who want him are the Quebec
Liberals. It started out good . . . there he was, a
young loyal Mulroney cabinet minister on his way
up. But then Brian left and Charest went for the
leadership and his party said, "No, we don't want
ya Jean, you're from Quebec. Go away. We're
going with the cello player from Vancouver." So
they went with Kim Campbell who turned out to be
the political equivalent of anthrax.

And when it was all over, the only ones standing
were Charest and some crazy person from New
Brunswick nobody had ever heard of before. So

Charest became the leader. But let's face it, when his turn finally came, they weren't exactly lining up around the block for the job. Squeegee kids were turning it down. But he worked hard, rebuilt the party, led twenty MPs back into the House. And what's his reward? A bunch of Tories out West wanna get rid of him "'cuz he's from Quebec."

Jean: with friends like those you might as well be hanging out with Liberals. Take the job in Quebec. Become a Liberal. Granted you'll have to become a lot more right wing, but hey, you get to hang out in your own province, and you might actually save the entire country while you're at it. Or you could end up losing it all to Lucien Bouchard. But at least you tried. And the country's worth it. And if it doesn't work out, you could always join the NDP.

Senator With a Mission

(First aired March 16, 1998)

It's been suggested lately by a number of irresponsible members of the media that Canadian senators do nothing but sit around and live high on the hog at taxpayers' expense. Well nothing could be further from the truth. Take Tory senator Pat Carney for example. Pat Carney is on a mission. She has stumbled upon a horrible injustice and she will not rest until this wrong has been righted.

Pat Carney checked into the Citadel Hotel in Ottawa recently. She went down for breakfast, and in the lobby they have free continental breakfast. They've got free fruit salad there, free muffins, free croissants, all laid out for the taking. But Pat didn't want fruit salad. She didn't want a muffin. Pat wanted bagels and not just any old bagels . . . Pat wanted low-fat bagels, and she wanted them for free.

So Pat Carney wrote to all of our parliamentarians, including the prime minister of Canada, complaining that they wouldn't give her a low-fat bagel, and that the free food provided should be labelled "Warning: This food is dangerous for your health." She wrote every member of the House of Commons. Every member of the Canadian Senate. More than four hundred letters have gone out.

Nothing can stop her. She's like Martin Luther of the free breakfast buffet set. She is trying to use the office of the Senate to force a private company to give her free food. But you have to understand, she's a senator. On her planet everything is free.

And I think it's obvious, she deserves special treatment. Luckily we live in Canada, where those treatments are covered under universal health care. And sadly, while Pat may have to pay two bucks for that bagel, we can all rest assured she won't have to pay a cent for the psychiatrist.

Update: Pat Carney had the guts to try and spoof this rant. She said she was simply attempting in a light-hearted way to encourage parliamentarians to promote heart-healthy food in their workplaces — airplanes, hotels, parliamentary functions. Who said satire was dead?

Flag Flap

(First aired March 23, 1998)

I'm a little bit confused. The Reform Party claims to be a grass-roots party. They came along to offer a fiscally-responsible alternative to the old guard parties. They promised to bring proper decorum back to the House of Commons. They promised to listen to the people of Canada.

Now did I miss it or did they say the way to do this is to load a bunch of MPs in a car, cut off the roof, paint it with Canadian flags and bomb around Parliament Hill like a bunch of drunks at the Grey Cup parade? No wonder Quebec wants to separate. They want to get the hell away from them.

The Reform Party is outraged because they think they should be able to sing "O Canada" in parliament whenever they want. In the middle of Question Period, if they don't like what someone is saying, they want to be able to stand up and sing a song . . . and wave a flag . . . so nothing gets done . . . and if you wanna stop them . . . then you're un-Canadian.

They think this is grass roots.

Well, I hate to tell you Preston, but in case you forget, people in the grass roots have jobs, real jobs. And if people with real jobs dealt with their problems at work by standing up whenever they wanted and singing "O Canada", they'd be unemployed. And Preston, when you're in Question Period, your job is to ask questions, not to sing songs . . . that's why it's called Question Period . . . not Play Group.

See Canadians aren't as stupid as we look. Canadians like the maple leaf and "O Canada" because they're important symbols. Preston likes them because they can be used as weapons. Now *that's* un-Canadian!

Bitter Pill

(First aired March 30, 1998)

We have a health care system now where in some provinces if you go to the doctor and get a mole removed it'll cost you a hundred bucks. But hang on, there's good news. If it turns out to be cancer you get the hundred bucks back.

And despite this, at the big Liberal convention last week the Liberals got some shocking news from their party pollster. He announced to the rank and file—and it was news to them—that after massive polling he figures that health care is the new number one priority of the Canadian people. Wow . . . I can see why the Liberals pay this guy the big bucks. He's like Sherlock Holmes. That's quite the bomb he dropped. Right up there with . . . when people get thirsty, they drink water.

So this is why after five years of cutting and slashing three and a half billion dollars in health care, the Liberals are not going ahead with their plans to cut another one and a half billion dollars from health care. 'Cuz now they want to be seen as pro-health care. They're kinda like a guy who spends five years beating a dog with a stick then says "Tomorrow I won't hit 'im with the stick, I'll just scare 'im a little. 'Cuz you know, I'm pro-dog."

Well the Liberals can say whatever they want, but they better do more than just stop cutting. 'Cuz balanced books or not, health care is going to be the dog that turns around and bites 'em right where it hurts.

Charles is Fifty

(First aired November 23, 1998)

I've never been a big fan of the monarchy, but man, I feel bad for Prince Charles. I mean the guy was in diapers when he first realized that some day he was going to be king, and the way things are going, by the time it finally happens he'll be in diapers again. The guy just turned fifty and he's still not the king.

But oh, mumsy threw quite the party hey, invited everyone who was anyone. Except Camilla. Who Charles says he loves more than anybody else in the world. So what did he do? He left her home "'cuz Mom said." I can see if Mom doesn't like your date, not bringing her around the house in grade eleven. But usually by the time the grade twelve grad rolls around you're pretty well going out with whoever you want to go out with. C'mon Charles, you're half a century old. Time to stop sucking up to Mom.

It's not like she's doing him any favours. She's not going anywhere. Let's face it—those women live forever. His own grandmother was doing the twist at his birthday party. She's like 106, she's bionic, but God love her, she looks like she's got another forty years in her.

Charles, if you want to be king start acting like one. Marry whoever the hell you want and tell Mom if she doesn't like it, she's going to the Home.